Moses on Leadership

A Qur'anic Narration

Iqbal J. Unus

First Edition November 2014

ISBN-13: 978-1449545598
ISBN-10: 1449545599

Printed in the U.S.A.

DEDICATION

To leadership in all of us.

ACKNOWLEDGMENTS

This short book owes much to the opportunities afforded to me to experience, exercise and teach leadership at various levels in Muslim faith-based organizations. For advice, access to resources and support, my thanks go to the leadership at Islamic Society of North America (ISNA), International Institute of Islamic Thought (IIIT), and Alwaleed Center for Muslim-Christian Understanding (ACMCU).

ADVICE

It is the practice of Muslims to say 'Peace be upon him' (Arabic: *alayhi al-salam*) when the name of any prophet – Moses and Aaron, for example – is mentioned. Muslims also remember the Majesty of God when they say Glorified and Exalted be He (Arabic: *Subhanahu wa Ta'la*) when the name of God is mentioned.

CONTENTS

"Go You to Pharaoh, for he had indeed transgressed all bounds." (Musa) *said: "O my Lord! Expand me my breast; Ease my task for me; and remove the impediment from my speech. So they may understand what I say: And give me a Minister from my family, Harun, my brother; Add to my strength through him, And make him share my task: That we may celebrate Your praise without stint, And remember You without stint: For You are He that ever watches us."* (Allah) *said: "Granted is your prayer, O Musa!"*

(Qur'an: Ta Ha, 20:24-36)

PREFACE

This short book cannot claim to be a guide to the complex human behavior that constitutes leadership. Far from it, it is simply intended to draw our attention to the historical and ever so ageless wisdom that is divinely inspired and communicated to mankind through the prophets and messengers of the divine Creator. The Prophet Moses (may peace be upon him) is one of those messengers who are distinguished by the way both the Old Testament and the Qur'an chronicle his life and his response to events that have influenced the religious practices of all three Abrahamic faiths.

This short book draws on a specific phase in the life of Moses as narrated in the Qur'an. It makes no attempt to compare this narration with Biblical versions of the same.

Leadership is not only a complex phenomenon, but it also encompasses a wide spectrum of the leader's personality traits and characteristics that help influence the individual and collective behavior of people who are led. Among these is the ability to communicate, to function as a team, and to delegate. The

Qur'anic narration of this phase of Moses' life provides us an opportunity to examine and ponder on these particular aspects of effective and purposeful leadership.

A number of books address the life of Moses and lessons that may be learned from it. As may be expected, the Qur'anic narration that is the subject of this short book is open to multiple interpretations, and a vast spectrum of meanings are embedded in the selected text. This work is narrowly focused on a few specific aspects of leadership, without any attempt to touch upon the various in-depth interpretations and meaning that more extensive and scholarly works offer. Nor does this work address the vast expanse of ideas in the selected aspects of leadership - just a few that may not have been explored elsewhere.

Needless to say, there is much else in the life of Moses that offers moral, spiritual and practical guidance to aspiring and proven leaders and managers. Scriptural texts are best studied seeking answers to questions, because their fundamental purpose is to guide the seeker. Leaders and managers will be well advised to study the life of Moses with such questions in mind as may relate to their own experiences and needs. They will not be disappointed in the wisdom and insight they gain to guide them towards fulfillment and success in their personal and professional lives.

On a side note, those interested in the Biblical version of this subject may find David Baron's "Moses on Management: 50 Leadership Lessons from the Greatest Manager of All Time" useful. Those interested in the impact of Moses on American life may find Bruce Feiler's "America's Prophet: How the Story of Moses Shaped America" a worthwhile reading. Needless to say, this short book does not draw upon either of these works.

Lastly, since the Qur'anic narration about Moses and Aaron addresses Moses as Musa (pronounced Moosa) and Aaron as Harun (pronounced Haroon), I have chosen to keep the Qur'anic names instead of Biblical names in translations of Qur'anic verses, just as I have chosen to keep Allah as God's name.

1 MOSES THE LEADER

THE Qur'an relates the story of the Prophets Moses and Aaron in several different Surahs (chapters), including Surah Ta Ha from verse 24 to verse 36. In each instance, the story highlights one or more aspects of their role and actions as appropriate to the Qur'anic message at that point. When we bring together this revealed knowledge about the two prophets, we discover the full story including key principles of communication, teamwork and delegation - all vital elements of effective leadership.

Command to Moses

In Surah Ta Ha, God commanded Moses to confront Pharaoh, the powerful and oppressive king of the time, saying:

> "Go You to Pharaoh, for he has indeed transgressed all bounds." (Ta Ha, 20:24)

At this stage, God's command was directed to Moses alone as an individual. Moses recognized this to be a great challenge and a formidable task to accomplish. His response to this assignment provides many lessons in leadership. These form the roots of important contemporary concepts related to communication, teamwork and delegation.

Asking for God's Help

In response to God's command, Moses first asked for God's help to enhance his capabilities and enable him to succeed in completing the assigned task. His plea for help represents the hallmark of a great leader, full of humility and dependent on His Lord for success.

> "(Musa) said: 'O my Lord! Expand for me my breast; Ease my task for me;'
> "(Ta Ha, 20:25-26)

Recognizing One's Limitations

Next, he took an inventory of the skills required for the job, assessed his own skills, and recognized his limitations. It is critical for the success of a mission to understand what skills are needed and to identify one's own strengths and weaknesses in the context of what is needed. Confident leaders do not shy away from confronting their limitations.

Immediately, Moses recognized that his communication skills were not as effective as they should be. He asked God to remove the difficulty he had in speaking effectively.

"And remove the impediment from my speech." (Ta Ha, 20:27)

Elsewhere, the Qur'an refers to Moses' request as follows:

"My breast will be straitened. And my speech may not go (smoothly): so send unto Harun..." (Al Shu'ara, 26:13)

In stating his requests to God, Moses reveals his pragmatic approach and his ability to assess potential problems. He shows an awareness of his own limitations - an exemplary quality for a good leader. With the difficulties and limitations in mind, he proposes a solution: form a team with his brother Aaron to do the job, with the teammate complementing the leader's skills.

Even though there are many lessons in the life story of Moses, the short chapters that follow focus on only three aspects of leadership: communication, teambuilding, and delegation.

2 MOSES THE COMMUNICATOR

Moses made the request to *"remove the impediment from my speech"* for a reason which illustrates a profound principle - in fact, the essence - of communication, His reason was:

> "So they may understand what I say:"
> (Ta Ha, 20:28)

He did not ask for removing the impediment in his speech so that he could speak better or more impressively. Instead he asked God to remove the impediment from his speech so that those who listened to him could understand him. This is the core of communication, that the receiver of the message should understand the message as it was intended to be understood. Communication takes place, not when the sender sends the message but when the receiver receives it and ascribes meaning to it.

To communicate with desired results, one should not become too absorbed in one's own abilities as speaker or presenter, but should focus on the anticipated interpretation and understanding of the message by the intended receiver or receivers. One should direct improvement in one's ability to communicate clear understanding of the message one intends to convey.

This principle can be extended to other areas of human activity. Any work should be judged not by how well we did it, but how well it benefited those affected by it. In other words, all our actions should be result oriented, and one should, of course, intend the result to be beneficial. The Prophet Muhammad (may peace be upon him) is reported to have said: *"People are dependents of God; the closest to Him are the most useful to His dependents."* (Sahih Muslim)

One must prepare for effective communication in advance of the occasion for such communication, as Moses did in this instance.

Focusing on Effective Communication

Further, this principle of communicating to be understood applies to all levels and all categories of communication, from a one-on-one personal talk to a small group discussion, to a major speech addressing a large audience. In each case, communication must have a purpose that is directed to achieving results – persuading, motivating, commanding, or instructing, for example. In this instance, Moses was seeking compliance of Pharaoh to

God's order, so he was focused on making sure that Pharaoh understood the order he was conveying, regardless of how well he could articulate it.

One may also note here the characteristics of the audience. God ordered Moses to go to Pharaoh because he had *"transgressed all bounds,"* and at the same time specified a way of dealing with this ruler.

> "But speak to him mildly; perchance he may take warning or fear (God)." (Ta Ha, 20:44)

The lesson here is that both the content of our communication and its medium, i.e. the manner of its delivery, should fit the receiver of the message. Further, sometimes the right way to deal with a harsh and unrepentant receiver is not in a like manner but in quite the opposite manner, speaking to him *"mildly"* as in this case. The essence of communication is getting a message across, not getting even.

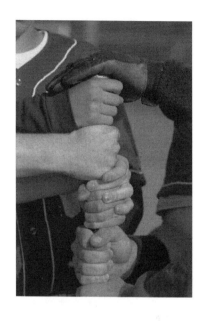

3 MOSES THE TEAMBUILDER

Moses also understood the need for building a team. He recognized that he needed to complement his own abilities in order to succeed. That led to the next part of his response to God's command to confront Pharaoh.

> "And give me a Minister from my family, Harun, my brother;" (Ta Ha, 20:29-30)

Moses wished to recruit his brother as a team member in order to strengthen his own abilities and efforts, and to enhance his own skills

> "Add to my strength through him," (Ta Ha, 20:31)

Adding strength is not only having more energy to do something, but also taking advantage of the synergy in doing it. Synergy makes the work of two halves better than that of one whole (persons or processes or resources).

For the team to be effective, Moses expected his teammate to participate in carrying out the task, and not be a mere bystander.

"And make him share my task:" (Ta Ha, 20:32)

Working as a Team

Leaders who are unsure of themselves often recruit teammates who are less qualified than themselves in order to avoid being challenged in areas of their own weaknesses. Effective leaders, however, are confident of themselves and focus their efforts on accomplishing the mission. Hence, they seek people who will complement them competently in areas where they perceive themselves to be weak or lacking. Moses asked for someone he knew to be capable, his own brother Aaron, for specific reasons, not mere familiarity or favor.

The Qur'an brings to our attention one important reason why Moses asked God to assign Aaron to help him.

"And my brother Harun - he is more eloquent in speech than I: so send him with me as a helper, to confirm (and strengthen) me: For I fear they may accuse me of falsehood." (Al Qasas, 28:34)

An effective team is characterized by teammates whose skills complement those of the leader as well as of other members of the team. As we saw earlier, Moses feared that his speech might not be adequate for the task at hand; so he asked for someone he considered to be better in that particular area. This is the mark of an effective leader. Further, Moses asserted that the purpose of forming a team was not merely to reduce one's workload, but to get help and strength from one another, as we have noted above. Such a team is directed to a purpose and to meet a challenge, which, in this case, carried the risk of being accused of promoting falsehoods.

Mission Orientation

A team should have a mission towards which it directs all its efforts. The success of the team is dependent upon the clarity of that mission and upon the degree to which all members are committed to accomplishing it. Moses clarified his team's mission.

"That we may celebrate Your praise without stint, and remember You without stint: For You are He that ever watches us." (Ta Ha, 20:33-35)

One must note the relationship between praise (*tasbih*) and remembrance (*zikr*) on the one hand and accomplishing an objective - community building, for example – on the other. The mission to which Moses and Aaron were directed was the release of the Israelites from the clutches of Pharaoh. To them that mission encompassed the praise and remembrance of God, for all action carried out to establish His Will would indeed amount to His praise and remembrance. Praising God and remembering Him establish the moral bearings that crystallize our mission and move us to accomplish it. On the other hand, exerting ourselves to accomplishing our purpose and mission within God's commandments and boundaries is an indisputable way to praise and remember Him.

Mission orientation is also crucial for the success of the mission. The leader and followers both must expend their energies in actions and activities that are in harmony with their mission and avoid actions and activities that will detract them. Moses and Aaron were both focused on their mission in whatever they said or did.

Legitimacy of the Request

God established the legitimacy of Moses' request - and approach - by granting what he had requested.

> "Granted is your prayer, O Musa!" (Ta Ha, 20:36)

The Qur'an also refers to the acceptance of Moses' request elsewhere.

> "(Before this), We sent Musa the Book, and appointed his brother Harun with him as Minister; " (Al Furqan, 25:35)

Emphasis on the Team

It is very important to note that, having granted the request of Moses to assign Aaron as his teammate, God stresses that relationship in numerous verses in the

Qur'an. The team of Moses and Aaron is presented to us as one unit, addressed by God as such and recognized by others as such.

> "Then after them sent We Musa and Harun to Pharaoh and his chiefs with Our Signs..."(Yunus, 10:75).

> "We inspired Musa and his brother with this Message:... "(Yunus, 10:87).

God said:

> "Accepted is your prayer (O Musa and Harun)! ..." (Yunus, 10:89)

> "And We commanded: Go you both, to the people who have rejected Our Signs:... "(Al Furqan, 25:36)

> "Again, (of old,) We bestowed Our favor on Musa and Harun .....'Peace and salutation to Moses and Aaron.' " (Al Saffat, 37:114...120)

Similarly the Qur'an uses the dual form to refer to the two prophets in Surah Ta Ha,

Ayahs 42-49, again highlighting the fact that they were a team.

Acting as a Team

Moses and Aaron acted as a team. The words *"They said"* and *"We fear"* in the verse that follows, indicate a process of active consultation between the two of them. In an effective team, each teammate plays a part. The leader's job is to determine which teammate is suited to play which part and when.

> "They (Musa and Harun) said: 'Our Lord! We fear lest he hasten with insolence against us, or lest he transgress all bounds.' " (Ta Ha, 20:45)

Recognition of the Team

Aaron was a significant part of the team, not merely an attendant to Moses. Pharaoh recognized this fact; the Qur'an tells us.

"(When this message was delivered, Pharaoh) said: 'Who then, O Musa, is the Lord of you two?' " (Ta Ha, 20: 49)

The sorcerers in the court also referred, not to the Lord of Moses alone, but to the Lord of Moses and Aaron, recognizing the latter as a significant partner of the former.

"Then did the sorcerers fall down, prostrate in adoration, saying: 'We believe in the Lord of the Worlds, the Lord of Musa and Harun.' " (Al Shu'ara, 26:46-48)

The Qur'anic narration does not include any incidence of Aaron speaking in the court of Pharaoh, even though Aaron was clearly part of the team and was selected because he was *more eloquent in speech than I*, as Moses said. What is clear is that the team of Moses and Aaron had a leader – Moses – who, benefiting from the capability and strength of his teammate, exercised leadership, as team leaders should.

The effective of a team is dependent on the role of teammates just as much as it does on their leader. Aaron was an effective teammate for Moses. He played his part but he let the leader lead.

4 MOSES THE DELEGATOR

When God asked Moses to leave his people for forty days, Moses put them under the supervision of Aaron. In other words, he delegated the leadership of the community and the management of its affairs to his teammate. In doing so, Moses defined the delegated task in broad terms as follows:

> ".... And Moses had charged his brother Harun (before he went up): 'Act for me amongst my people: Do right, and follow not the way of those do mischief.' " (Al A'raf, 7:142).

Moses illustrated three important aspects of effective delegation in this case.

First, he delegated broadly but clearly by charging Aaron to act for him amongst his people. Second, he clarified his expectation - the intended objective - by asking Aaron to do right. Third, he placed appropriate limits on the delegated authority by asking Aaron not to follow the way of those who do mischief.

Thus delegation, from this perspective, consists of defining (a) what is the task, (b) what should be the end result, and (c) what are the boundaries within which the task should be performed and results accomplished? The interaction between the one delegating (Moses) and the one who is delegated (Aaron) is circumscribed by factors that are often neglected in the process of delegation – responsibility, authority, and priority.

The Responsibility

When Moses returned to his people and found that Aaron had been unable to prevent his people from being misled by Samiri, he was upset. He held Aaron accountable but assumed responsibility himself, illustrating one of the most basic rules of delegation, that <u>one cannot delegate responsibility; one can only delegate authority</u>.

> "Musa prayed: 'O my Lord! Forgive me and my brother! Admit us to Your mercy! For You are the Most Merciful of those who show mercy!' " (Al A'raf, 7:151)

Moses asked for forgiveness for himself - for getting angry, and for being unable to fulfill his responsibility - as well as forgiveness for his brother - for his seeming failure in his delegated task, which was *"Do right..."*. He asked for forgiveness for himself **first**, which speaks to his consciousness of his own role as the team leader, and the one responsible. As an effective leader, Moses went further and identified himself with his people and their role in this situation.

> ".... He prayed: 'O my Lord! If it had been Your Will You could have destroyed, long before, both them and me: would You destroy us for the deeds of the foolish ones among us? This is no more than Your trial: by it You cause whom You will to stray, and You lead whom you will into the right path...' " (Al A'raf, 7:155).

The Authority

God teaches us another principle of delegation in this story - that, one to whom a task is delegated must be given sufficient authority and resources to carry it out - when He says:

> "Then We sent Musa and his brother Harun, with Our Signs and authority manifest,... "(Al Mu'minun, 23:45)

As in the verse above, so in the verse below, God refers to the two prophets together and underscores two additional principles of delegation. These are: those delegated a task must be supported (*We are with you*), and they must be given a hearing and feedback as necessary (*will listen (to your call)*).

"God said: 'By no means! Proceed then both of you, with Our Signs; We are with you, and will listen (to your call).'" (Al Shu'ara, 26:15)

This message of support and assistance is repeated elsewhere in the Qur'an.

"So go forth, both of you, to Pharaoh, and say: 'We have been sent by the Lord and Cherisher of the Worlds.' " (Al Shu'ara, 26:16)

"He said: 'We will certainly strengthen your arm through your brother, and invest you both with authority, so they shall not be able to touch you: with Our Signs shall you triumph - you two as well as those who follow you.'" (Al Qasas, 28:35)

The Priority

When Moses was away to meet God, Samiri caused a rebellion among the people against the legitimately delegated leadership of Aaron, and misled them into deviating from the worship of God to the worship of a calf. When Moses returned to his people and found them misled, he asked Aaron what prevented him from following his orders when he saw his people doing wrong. After asking him not be angry with him, (Aaron) replied:

> ".. Truly I feared lest you should say, 'You have caused a division among the Children of Israel, and you did not respect my word!' "(Ta Ha, 20:94)

The environment Aaron faced, when Moses had gone away, was not the same. Therefore, we see in this exchange between the two brothers and prophets that their priorities differed. The priority of Aaron was to maintain unity among the Children of Israel. The priority of Moses was higher - to maintain the purity of worship among the people.

This exchange points to the fact that a hierarchy of priorities may be at play in delegation. Both the team leader and the team mate(s) must be cognizant of the role of such priorities.

Thus, to ensure effective delegation, a responsible leader provides a clear description of the assignment and its bounds, allocates necessary resources and authority, and offers sufficient freedom to achieve results.

There is one more message in this narration. When Moses returned, he did not rush to condemn anyone. He gave even Samiri, whose guilt was established beyond any doubt, an opportunity to explain his action before arriving at the conclusion of expelling him.

"(Musa) said: 'What then is your case. O Samiri?' " (Ta Ha, 20:95)

Such should be the exercise of fairness and justice even when the conclusion may seem to be obvious.

5 ONE MORE LESSON

Moses exemplified the ideal candidate for an assignment, one who could be expected to perform and achieve. A critical episode in his life illustrates that the person to be so chosen should have two major characteristics: competence and trustworthiness. These are the qualities that were apparent in Moses when the elderly man whose daughters he helped at the water well during his journey in the land of Madyan hired him.

> "Said one of the (damsels): 'O my (dear) father! Engage him on wages: truly the best of men for you to employ is the (man) who is strong and trusty.'"
> (Al Qasas, 28:26)

While many other characteristics may be relevant to the task at hand, strength, in its broadest sense, and trustworthiness, with all is its associations, are indeed what leaders search for.

Strength relates to competence and skills needed to perform the task at hand. While physical prowess may be called for in some situations, in other circumstances strength may mean intellectual ability or technical proficiency.

Similarly trustworthiness includes a broad spectrum of qualities that leaders and employers seek, including honesty, loyalty, and truthfulness, for example. Often trustworthiness may be more desirable than strength, because while competence and skills may be acquired through learning and training, honesty and truthfulness are generally part of one's character and in-bred through good upbringing.

6 CONCLUSION

The story of Moses and Aaron played out on a historical stage that was undoubtedly different from that in modern life. In contemporary social organizations from the family to the nation state, new modes of thinking of, and relating to, one another have led to new ways of leading people and managing organizational enterprises. Yet at the core, human instincts and behavior, ingenuity and initiative, and the struggle to discover the right course of action, all remain rooted in the immutable nature of the human person. That is why divinely inspired guidance is always contemporary and modern.

For people of faith, with their belief system rooted in a divine scripture, leadership lessons from the life of Moses will deepen their understanding of contemporary concepts in personal and organizational behavior. In a manner of speaking, people of faith are better able to internalize contemporary theories and models when they can relate them to their spiritual and moral underpinnings.

The story of Moses and Aaron, even in this brief discourse, offers us valuable lessons in leadership and the art of working together. In these lessons, we discover the scriptural origins of present-day concepts in organizational behavior, whose understanding and practice will enhance our ability to perform well and achieve satisfaction, God Willing.

ABOUT THE AUTHOR

Dr. Iqbal Unus [Ph.D., Emory University 1977] has focused his professional career on the evolving Muslim presence in America, gaining distinctive insight into its growth. He is associated with the International Institute of Islamic Thought, and has served as secretary general of the Islamic Society of North America, and member of its Board. He has published several articles in Islamic Horizons, a book chapter in *The Muslims' Place in the American Public Square*, and two children's books, as well as abridged *Apostasy in Islam: An Historical and Scriptural Analysis*, and edited *Muslim American Life: Reflections and Perspectives*.

Made in the USA
Middletown, DE
20 November 2014